Thinking of Mom

by M.O. Lufkin
Illustrated by Nina Khalova

Published in the United States by Literary Mango, Inc.

Little Neck, New York. First edition, 2017.

Literary Mango

www.literarymango.com

Discounts are available on quantity purchases by corporations, associations and others. For details, contact us through the website above.

Author: M.O. Lufkin

Illustrator: Nina Khalova

Editor: Jody Mullen

Summary: Illustrations and text tell a tale of loss as Dad helps Ella find happiness again after losing Mom.

Paperback ISBN 978-1-946844-03-3

Hardcover ISBN 978-1-946844-04-0

Mom helped Ella brush her teeth

And made her bed up nice and neat.

She helped her dress in matching clothes

And gently wiped her mouth and nose.

She took her to the park to play,

Made lunch and dinner every day,

And tucked her into bed each night,
With goodnight kisses, and hugs so tight.

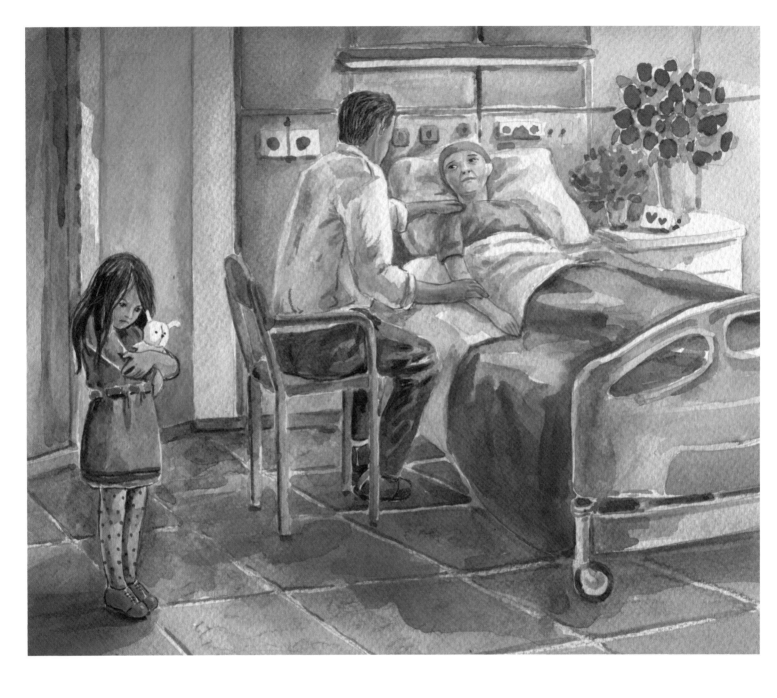

But then it happened, Mom got sick.

It made Ella so mad, she'd punch and kick.

Mom couldn't help her brush her teeth,

Or match her clothes for the week.

She couldn't take her out to play,

And Ella wanted to run away.

And then, when Dad said Mom was gone,
Ella didn't know how she'd go on.

She didn't want to say goodbye.
All she could do was sit and cry.

Though Dad was helpful and so sweet,

Poor Ella couldn't sleep or eat.

When it came time to go to bed,
She'd stay up late and cry instead.

So Dad said "Let's go for a walk.
We'll get some air, and we can talk."

And Dad said he was feeling blue.
He missed Mom's hugs and kisses too.

He missed her smile, her laugh, her eyes,
And sometimes, even Daddy cries.

When life feels tough and so unfair,
He shuts his eyes and sees her there.

At night, he sees her in a dream.
She's gotten well-eating ice cream!

She's praising Ella for being good,
And doing what good mothers would.

Mom gives him strength, both day and night.
She helps him know what's fair and right.

So Ella went to bed that night
And closed her eyes really tight.

She thought of Mom and how she was,
And thought of Dad and what he does.

Then Ella slept, and Mom was there!
She had ice cream and said she'd share!

Mom said to Ella that she missed her,
And Ella smiled and hugged and kissed her.

She slept all night, and that next day,
She found her tears had gone away!

She dressed herself, and, feeling glad,
She went outside to play with Dad.

In all the things they say and do,
Ella and Dad know Mom's with them, too.

Discussion Questions

Why was Ella so sad and mad?

What did Ella miss about Mom?

What did Dad do to help Ella feel better?

Can you think of some ways to remember someone you don't see anymore?

Who can help you when you're feeling sad and missing someone you love?

How can you help others when they are feeling sad?

What could you do to make a person you miss proud of you?

Try These Children's Books

Animals Can Sing by M.O. Lufkin is a fun story where the reader goes on a short adventure in the woods. You'll visit with the bees, a wolf pup and other animals as you go deeper into a mystical forest. Told in rhyme, this delightful and fun children's picture book comes to life with a musical score printed on the last page that you can sing to, while enjoying the beautiful landscape illustrations of natural scenery that enhance your literary journey and captivate the imaginations of young readers.

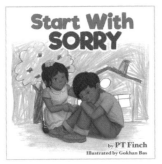

In *Start With Sorry* by P.T. Finch, Three-year-old Luna loves to spend time with her older brother, Asher, and she wants to do everything he does. But when they sit down to draw pictures together, Luna feels upset that she can't do everything he can do. When she reacts in anger, Asher is sad and doesn't want to color with her anymore. With Mommy's help, Luna learns how to make amends for hurting her brother's feelings. Kids love this story, and adults appreciate the valuable lesson it teaches about empathy for others.

Buddy's New Friend is P.T. Finch's second children's picture book in a series about siblings Luna and Asher. Their pet cat, Buddy is lonely during the day when everyone is away at school and work, so the family goes to a local animal shelter to find him a new friend. In addition to curing Buddy's loneliness, the siblings learn a valuable lesson in empathy when they choose an older dog among swarms of cute puppies. Will Buddy and his new friend get along, or will they fight like cats and dogs? Read the book to find out!

www.literarymango.com

Literary Mango

CPSIA information can be obtained at www.ICGtesting.com
Printed in the USA
LVIW01n2252010817
543490LV00001B/2